Java Programming

Advanced Features and Programming Techniques

(Learn the Basics of Java Programming Without Any Experience)

Alfonso Floyd

Published By **Kate Sanders**

Alfonso Floyd

Java Programming: Advanced Features and Programming Techniques (Learn the Basics of Java Programming Without Any Experience)

ISBN 978-1-9992844-3-5

No part of this guidebook shall be reproduced in any form without permission in writing from the publisher except in the case of brief quotations embodied in critical articles or reviews.

Legal & Disclaimer

The information contained in this book is not designed to replace or take the place of any form of medicine or professional medical advice. The information in this book has been provided for educational & entertainment purposes only.

The information contained in this book has been compiled from sources deemed reliable, and it is accurate to the best of the Author's knowledge; however, the Author cannot guarantee its accuracy and validity and cannot be held liable for any errors or omissions. Changes are periodically made to this book. You must consult your doctor or get professional medical advice before using any of the suggested remedies, techniques, or information in this book.

Upon using the information contained in this book, you agree to hold harmless the Author from and against any damages, costs, and expenses, including any legal fees potentially resulting from the application of any of the information provided by this guide. This disclaimer applies to any damages or injury caused by the use and application, whether directly or indirectly, of any advice or information presented, whether for breach of contract, tort, negligence, personal injury, criminal intent, or under any other cause of action.

You agree to accept all risks of using the information presented inside this book. You need to consult a professional medical practitioner in order to ensure you are both able and healthy enough to participate in this program.

TABLE OF CONTENTS

Chapter 1: Defining & Designing Your Data

Anything in this universe can be represented by data. Your name, age, gender, what car you drive, what city you live in, country, planet, galaxy, and so on. They can all be data.

To design great apps, games, or any other digital tool you can think of, the fine details that comprise them will have to be represented by the data types you choose.

Choosing your Data Types

There are two questions to ask yourself when you're designing data to represent something.

First, identify what type of data you can define that 'thing'. It can be an Integer, Number, Boolean (yes/no type things), String, or some other data type. For example, your name is a String (a sequence of letters), your Age is a Number, and you live in a City or

Town. Your city of town has a name - another String.

Second, identify whether or not that thing is a part of a whole; included in a larger thing. For example, you may have a friend named Jamie. She's included in a list of your friends. We'll cover this more later on; just keep the concept of 'parts belonging to a larger whole' in mind.

Representing your information as a Data Type

In most programming languages, you can often define data in one line of code. Here we define your data as a Global Variable - meaning this editable line of data is available throughout your program.

JAVA-00: Quick Important notes about Java code

A Java Class File

Classes will be explained more in detail later in JAVA-02. But for now, start your Java code with these next few lines of code:

```java
// ————————————————

import java.util.*;

import java.lang.*;

import java.io.*;

class ___ {

public static void main(String args[]) {

// CODE HERE

}

}

// ————————————————
```

By default, online compilers will have a similar code structure to the above. For now, just make sure you ONLY add code within the brackets by 'public static void main' (where the comments tell you to)

Also, make sure all three import lines above are in your code. Plenty of Java functionality is from these Java libraries.

NOTE:

if you use an online compiler we mentioned, fill in the blank line beside class into one of the below, depending on which site you've used:

Rextester (rextester.com): fill with 'Rextester'

CodeChef (www.codechef.com/ide): fill with 'Codechef'

Codepad: (doesn't support Java)

Ideone (https://ideone.com/): fill with 'Ideone'

JAVA-01a: A Glimpse of Java Code

Here are a few simple lines of code to help you feel more familiar with Java.

To complete the code, simply fill in the blanks with your own answers. Afterwards, copy-paste the code onto rextester.com, ideone.com, codechef.com, or any compiler of your choice. If you use any of the sites above, make sure to set the programming language to Java.

```java
import java.util.*;

import java.lang.*;

class Rextester

{

public static void main(String args[])

{

// Your name is a String

String name = "________";

// Your age is an Integer

int age = ___;

 // 'It's raining outside'

// This fact is a boolean: either true or false

boolean itsRaining = ___;

}
```

```
}
```

In the next chapter, we'll explain Java syntax and code in more detail. If necessary, feel free to read ahead, then come back to this code to finish it.

Further on, we'll look into more intermediate and advanced programming techniques and skills.

JAVA-01b: Defining & Designing your Data

JAVA Comments

In Java, comments are just the same as other common languages like C, C++, PHP, and even our own pseudocode.

Single-line comments start with two slashes (//) and end when the line breaks to the next line of code.

Multiple comment lines start with a slash and a star (/*) and end with the reverse: a star and a slash (*/).Often, multiple comment lines also start withstars (*) on each line.

Here's an example of a multi-line comment:

* This is a

* multi-line

* comment */

An Explanation for your Data

A good practice in defining your data is to make comments above the line of code that explains why you have your data the way it is.

One of the lines can be in the format of "_____ is a (Data Type)".

Here's an example, in Java:

//My Name is a String

String name = "Joseph";

Here are some more examples:

//My Age is an Integer

int age = 35;

//I live in a City or Town, with a Name

```java
// My city's name is a String

String city = "New York";

// I am either hungry or not

// My hunger status is a Boolean

boolean hungry = true;

// I either have a pet or I don't

// Whether or not I have a pet is a Boolean

boolean hasPet = false
```

Essential Java Syntax

Out of most programming languages out there, Java has one of the more strict code syntax.

Similar to other code such as C, C++, and PHP, lines of code in Java end with a semicolon (;). This is very important; Java programmers commonly have errors in their code just because their lines don't end with a semicolon.

Atomic Data in Java

Atomic data in Java is defined VERY strictly.

Booleans in Java are strictly lower case. If your booleans are all upper-case (TRUE), or first-letter uppercase (True), most Java compilers will report these as errors. So for booleans, stick with all lower-case letters. So either (true) or (false).

Strings in Java can only start and end with double parentheses ("). Do not use single parentheses (') to start and end strings. For example, "String" is a string, but 'String' is not.

Instead, single characters in Java start and end with single parentheses ('). For example, 'a' is a single character.

Floats in Java always end with the letter f. For example, some Floating Point Integers in Java can be 1.2f and 0.75f.

On the other hand, Java uses the data type Double to also represent decimal numbers. For example, 1.2 and 0.75 can be Doubles.

Java Data Definitions

Let's define some data in Java.

Luckily, the pseudocode we've used earlier follows a very similar syntax to what we use here with Java. You will have to define your data type once you code the data you want to store. However, Java uses distinct, case-sensitive words to define your data variables.

Chapter 2: Compound/Composite Data

From the last chapter's example, you can start to wonder that there just has to be a way to group a handful of data together. For example, your name, age, location, whether or not you have pets, etc.

Also, notice that an entire person can neither be a String, Number, Integer, nor Boolean. A person just holds too much data to be defined as either one of the above.

So what do we do?

What a Composite Data Structure is

From the previous example, you can think of all the data you've defined as small parts of a whole. But what is this "whole"?

Enter Composite Data.

A Composite Data structure includes many parts of data within it.

Those parts of the Composite could be whatever you wish to declare. Strings,

Integers, Booleans, Lists, and even other Composite Data.

Identify & Defining a Composite Data Structure

When you were asked earlier to define what type of data are you dealing with, what if you designed & defined data for an object that you couldn't identify as atomic data? What if it had plenty of characteristics? What if there was more depth in that object?

The key thing to remember in identifying composite data is depth. There are more parts to that 'thing' you were trying to define as data. If there's more to anything than just a name, number, or true/false switch, then it's probably going to be a composite data structure.

Object-Oriented Programming

Today, almost all of conventional programming is object-oriented.

This type of programming consists of two parts. The first part focuses on thoroughly defining compound data structures and procedures.

The second part executes the main procedure - while using the data structures and procedures defined in the first part.

So for example, you can define the data for a house, including its dimensions, cost, features, etc. This would be the first part of object-oriented programming. Afterwards, your main procedure could be to create ten red houses in one city block and twelve big blue houses in the next block. This would be the second part - your main procedure is based on whatever you've designed in the first part.

Object-Oriented Programming Explained Simply

Simply put, objects are created and initialized based on their respective classes.

Think of a data class as 'blueprints' to a house. It contains ALL the data a house would have, such as dimensions, materials, etc..

Think of an object as the actual house. When a house is created, it's based on the blueprints of a house. So when a data object is created it's based on its data class.

Why we have Object-Oriented Programming

From the previous chapters, our approach to programming was to use comments to describe what our data is. Each line of code, which then becomes procedural instructions to the computer, is literally defined by the description comments you've written.

So from a programmer's perspective, designing and developing apps becomes more descriptive in nature. Certain aspects of your app are actually data classes you describe, which are used to create data objects during program execution.

Constructors

Classes also have specific functions called constructors. Their main purpose is to create the actual data object based on its data class.

Programmers can also use constructors to set the components of their data classes.

Intermediate and Advanced Object-Oriented Programming

During the development process, programmers will have to figure out not just their data class designs, but how many different objects are created during program execution. For example: on a single game of PacMan, how many white dots will a game of PacMan have? How many ghosts? How many fruits?

We'll explain this more in detail later on. For now, just remember the basics of Object-Oriented Programming.

JAVA-02a: Compound/Composite Data

In Java, we define our composite data structures as Data Classes.

Java: an Object-Oriented Programming Language Only

As you can see, data structures classes form the foundation of Java code.

A java class file will always have its EXACT case-sensitive filename as one of its classes. At the very minimum, a java class file will have at least one class. For example, a java file named ClassOne.java will have a class named ClassOne.

ClassOne.java:

```
class ClassOne {

// code here

}
```

Here's how a data structure with two attributes would look like, including the Explanation Comments:

```
// Our class has:

// - an attribute variable (String)
```

// - another attribute variable (Integer)

class className {

String attribute1;

int attribute2;

}

Initializing a Java Object

To create an Object based on your Java class, it would be just like setting a Javavariable's initial data value. However, you'll be setting that variable as a new Object. This object will have the same data structure as the class you set it as.

For Java classes, there are a few special lines of code you'll need to create called a Constructor.

A defined constructor within a class will have the following structure:

public ExactClassName(datatype input) {

// insert any code here

}

Often times, the class constructor will be right below all of the attributes of that class.

Overall, initializing a Java object would look like the following notation:

ClassName OBJECTNAME = new ClassName();

The word 'new', along with the constructor for that class, initializes your object.

You've already defined that your object will have the data structure of whatever class you've assigned it to.

Accessing Class Attributes

This follows a similar structure to our PseudoCode.

To access a Class Attribute, you first have a variable object that has been assigned that Class structure. Then follow it up with a period (.), then the class attribute you want to access.

Let's say we have a class with two attributes in it:

```
class Class {

String attribute1;

int attribute2;

}
```

Next, let's recall setting object1 into a class:

```
Class object1 = new Class();
```

Then accessing object1's attributes would look like the following notation:

```
object1.attribute1

object1.attribute2
```

Can you guess what data type you end up with when you access these two class attributes? If you look at your data definition for your Class, you've defined the attributes for that class with specific data types. Therefore:

object1.attribute1 (this returns a String)

object1.attribute2 (this returns an Integer)

EXAMPLE:

Think about a book. A physical book that probably sits near your shelf. Let's start defining the Composite Data Structure for it.

First, let's use comments to describe what our our data will look like.

// A Book Has:

Now think of the little attributes a book has. Is the cover a Hardcover, Paperback, or something else? How many pages does it have? Is it a Fiction book or not? What's the title? Who's the Author? How much did that Book cost?

// A Book Has:

// - a Cover Type (String)

// - a Page Count (Integer)

// - a Title (String)

// - an Author Name (String)

// - a price (Number)

In Java, numbers with decimals can have either data type float or double. For now, let's go with double.

Now, let's design the Book Class in Java.

```java
class Book {

String coverType;

int pageCount;

String title;

String authorName;

double price;

}
```

For fun, let's also create a Harry Potter book object.

```java
Book harryPotter = new Book();
```

JAVA-02b: More Data Class Practice

Representing information as Data Classes

Let's take a person as an example. You are a Person. As a person, you're not JUST a name or number; you are comprised of a lot of data. A seemingly endless amount of data, rather. And so is everyone else.

The Elements that Comprise your Data

As an example of a Data Class (or just any Composite Data in general), let's define a person.

For now, let's start with the declaration.

//I am a PERSON

class Person{}

Similar to what you did earlier for defining basic data types, it's also best that you identify what your data class is comprised of.

For practice, use comments to describe what your data structure has.

Following the example code above, a Person has a Name and an Age as well. And so do you. Let's include those components:

```
//I am a PERSON

// A person has:

// - a name (string)

// - an age (number)

class Person{

String name;

int age;

}
```

Afterwards, we'll need the constructor for our data class. This is a special function used to create the data objects. For our Person class, we'll set the name and age as constructor inputs. So once a data objectis created, it will have its information defined.

```
//I am a PERSON
```

```
// A person has:

// - a name (string)

// - an age (number)

class Person{

String name;

int age;

// CONSTRUCTOR:

Person(String n, int a) {

this.name = n;

this.age = a;

}

}
```

A person very likely lives in a City. Oh but wait, a City isn't just a name is it? It's comprised of plenty of data as well. Hence, it can also be a data class, with its own components and its own constructor:

```java
//This is a CITY

// A City has:

// - a name (string)

// - a Latitude and Longitude (2 numbers)

// - a Population count (an integer, above 0)

class City {

String name;

float latitude;

float longitude;

int population;

// CONSTRUCTOR:

City(String n, float la,

float lo, int p) {

this.name = n;

this.latitude = la;

this.longitude = lo;
```

```
    this.population = p;

  }

}
```

Let's not forget about you. You probably live in some City, remember?

```
//I am a PERSON

// A person has:

// - a name (string)

// - an age (number)

// - a City they live in (Composite data City)

class Person{

String name;

int age;

City location;

// CONSTRUCTOR:

Person(String n, int a, City c) {
```

this.name = n;

this.age = a;

this.location = c;

}

}

(Notice what happened here. A data class that includes an object of another data class!)

JAVA Workshop for Ch. 2

Go to an IDE of your choice. You may also use online IDE's such as rextester.com, ideone.com, or www.codechef.com/ide. (if you do, make sure to set your Programming Language to Java).

If you use one of the online IDE's, you should see something similar to this:

```
// –––––––––––––––––

import java.util.*;

import java.lang.*;
```

```java
import java.io.*;

// INSERT MORE IMPORTS HERE

// INSERT MORE CLASSES HERE

class (whatever class name)

{

public static void main(String args[])

{

// INSERT CODE HERE

}

}
```

// ———————————————

Classy Kids

Design a data class definition for a car. Think carefully. What attributes would that car have?

Chapter 3: Data Initialization

Skilled programmers understand why they need to set, organize, and utilize their data and code in a sound manner. One of the most important reasons is to minimize, if not completely eliminate, bugs in the code.

Hence, this chapter and its accompanied sections aim to show you how to properly initialize your data.

There are key practical takeaways in this chapter:

- When accessing class fields, make sure you get the names right. This is why documentation is important!

- make sure you assign your variables and class fields with its correct data type

- When assigning variables as data objects, make sure to assign it with an existing data object

In the next few sections, you'll go through plenty of practice to see these takeaways first-hand.

JAVA-03: Data Initialization

Let's recall the Composite Data Structure of a Person (with no custom constructor):

```
// A person has:

// - a name (string)

// - an age (number)

// - a City they live in (Composite data City)

class Person {

String name;

int age;

City location;

}
```

We'll also create two Atomic Data pieces as the Time: two integers. The variables below will be inside the main() method:

int hour;

int minute;

You may have noticed one thing: You've defined what types of data you're dealing with - but we haven't created any people as data objects yet. Nor do we know what time it is!

Now we INITIALIZE our data. Now that we've defined what types of data we have, we then set our data for the first time.

Initializing Atomic Data

First, we'll set the time.

Let's say it's 8:30 PM. We'll set up our time as is.

To set data, most programming languages use the Equals (=) operator. Here, we'll do the same.

hour = 20;

minute = 30;

DON'T make this mistake…

But what if we tried to set hour and minute to another data type?

hour = "aaaa";

minute = "Typing a String on Purpose";

In Java, as well as most other programming languages, this code is not going to work. And in most cases, your code might not compile if your code expects your data to be a certain type. Earlier, we've set both hour and minute as Integers. Now, we're trying to set up those data as different data types.

You've set up your data as Integers - therefore, you need to initialize & change them as Integers.

Lesson learned: if you set up your data as a certain data type, unless you really know what you're doing, DO NOT try to set up that data as another data type!

Initializing Composite Data Structures

Now, let's define an actual Person using our data structure. There are FOUR KEY steps to do this:

STEP ONE:

Identify & describe a data object you're trying to create.

For practice, use comments to describe what that object is & what it's like. We'll use a friend of yours called Jamie, for example. We use comments to describe her:

// Jamie Denise is a person

// She has:

// - a name: Jamie Denise

// - an age: 19

// - a City she lives in: New York

STEP TWO:

Declare and initialize the type of composite data your object is.

Your data object is actually represented by the Composite Data in your program. In most languages, you declare that you have a new 'case' or instance of this object. Think of this step as "registering" your new object into your data program.

In this example, we INITIALIZE Jamie as a data object that HAS the Person Composite Data Structure:

// Jamie Denise is a person

Person Jamie = new Person();

Again, just like Atomic Data, we use the Equals (=) operator to assign variables with class instances.

STEP THREE:

For each data part that your Composite Data is made of, set those initial values.

In our example, do you remember Jamie's Attributes?

// Jamie Denise is a person

// She has:

// - a name: Jamie Denise

// - an age: 19

// - a City she lives in: New York

Now let's initialize each attribute onto our Data Object. You first need to identify the data object you're trying to reach. In this case, it's Jamie.

Next (and this is important!), identify which attribute you're planning to reach. Here's it's best to reference the Data Structure you've defined earlier:

```
class Person {

String name;

int age;

City location;

}
```

Let's set all three of Jamie's Attributes:

```
// Jamie Denise is a person

// She has:

// - a name: Jamie Denise

// - an age: 19

// - a City she lives in: New York

var Jamie = new Person();

Jamie.name = "Jamie"; // <— a "String": Remember?

Jamie.age = Nineteen;

CITY = NewYork;
```

Okay, we're done.

Hold on. The code is wrong. Why?

DON'T make these mistakes...

This line won't work:

```
Jamie.age = Nineteen;
```

Why?

Just a friendly reminder. Make sure the data type you're trying to set MATCHES the data type you've defined. In most programming languages, this is one of the most common mistakes programmers make. The word Nineteen is definitely not an Integer data type, nor is it a String (where's the "Quotation marks?"). However, 19 works.

Jamie.age = 19;

Also, This line doesn't work:

CITY = NewYork;

Why?

What's CITY? Did we mean Jamie's current CITY?

Remember to first identify the DATA OBJECT you're accessing. AND THEN that object's attributes.

Well, let's try that.

Jamie.CITY = NewYork;

This line won't work either. Why?

Because Jamie is a data object that follows the Person Composite Data Structure you've defined. And note how that Structure does NOT have any attributes named CITY in it.

Again, Remember to first identify the DATA OBJECT you're accessing. AND THEN access that object's correct attributes.

The Person Structure includes a separate City data structure, but it certainly isn't called CITY.

```
class Person {

var name: String?

var age: Int?

var location: City?

}
```

Oh, so the code should be:

```
Jamie.location = NewYork;
```

But you're missing one more thing. Where in your program is NewYork defined?

Well, that can be arranged. Let's recall the City data Structure and define the NewYork data object as well:

```
//This is a CITY

// A City has:

// - a name (string)

// - a Latitude and Longitude (2 numbers)

// - a Population count (an integer, above 0)

class City {

String name;

float latitude;

float longitude;

int population;

// CONSTRUCTOR:

// No custom constructor for this version
```

```
}
/*
//NewYork is a CITY

// NewYork has:

// - a name: "New York"

// - a Latitude and Longitude: 40.7127 and 74.0059

// - a Population count: 8406000

*/

City NewYork = new City();

NewYork.name = "New York";

NewYork.latitude = 40.7127f;

NewYork.longitude = 74.0059f;

NewYork.population = 8406000;
```

Chapter 4: Data Changes & Mutable States

In the previous chapters, you've defined some facts as data structures and even represented people and cities as data.

However, nothing ever stays the same in data.

Data changes over time - and it's important to keep track of how data values change and what they currently are.

Modifying your Defined Data Over Time

In reality, modifying the data values you've set in place is nearly similar to initializing them in the first place. In most programming languages, the same principles between initializing and updating data apply: identify the data you want to access, use the Equals Operator (=), and set the new data to another value, but usually the SAME data type you've originally set. So change data defined as Strings to other Strings, Integers to Integers, and so on.

JAVA-04a: Practice with Data Changes

Let's take a look at Jamie and New York from the past chapter. keep in mind that this is all within the main() method:

```
/*

//NewYork is a CITY

// NewYork has:

// - a name: "New York"

// - a Latitude and Longitude: 40.7127 and 74.0059

// - a Population count: 8406000

*/

City NewYork = new City();

NewYork.name = "New York";

NewYork.latitude = 40.7127;

NewYork.longitude = 74.0059;

NewYork.population = 8406000;
```

```
// Jamie Denise is a person

// She has:

// - a name: Jamie Denise

// - an age: 19

// - a City she lives in: New York

Person Jamie = new Person();

Jamie.name = "Jamie";

Jamie.age = 19;

Jame.location = NewYork;
```

So let's say 10 years have passed since we defined Jamie's data object onto our program. Since then, Jamie got married and changed her last name.

She also moved to Los Angeles. So how would her new Data Object look like?

You're essentially setting up all your changed data values to their new values. If you wanted to know what these values are, they would give you their current values.

// Jamie Walker is a person

// She has:

// - a name: Jamie Walker (changed from Jamie Denise)

// - an age: 29 (was 19)

// - a City she lives in: LosAngeles (was NewYork)

Jamie.name = "Jamie Walker";

Jamie.age = 29;

Jamie.location = LosAngeles;

and yes, make sure even LosAngeles is defined.

//LosAngeles is a CITY

// LosAngeles has:

// - a name: "Los Angeles"

// - a Latitude and Longitude: 34.0500 and 118.2500

// - a Population count: 3884000

City LosAngeles = new City();

LosAngeles.name= "Los Angeles";

LosAngeles.latitude = 34.0500;

LosAngeles.longitude = 118.2500;

LosAngeles.population = 3884000;

Keeping Track of your Defined Data

let's recall the Clock from a previous chapter:

int hour = 20;

int minute = 30;

At the moment, lets say it's definitely not 8:30 PM anymore, but 10 AM now.

How would the clock change? Easy:

hour = 10;

minute = 0;

Then three and a half hours pass. How would the clock change? Again, easy.

hour = 13;

minute = 30;

If you wanted the time afterwards, what would it be?

Not 8:30 PM, not 10 AM either. But 1:30 PM.

Here, you've been essentially setting up both your integers named HOUR and MINUTE to new values. If you wanted to know what these values are, they would give you their current values.

However, it's Important that you keep track of your changes. You MUST understand what the changes to your data have been - and you MUST determine whether or not those changes are what you want.

We stress this because one of the many traits a programmer needs to have (and be good at) is managing what happens to your data.

If you don't believe us, wait until you have your tech interviews for a programming position you're applying for...

JAVA-04b: More Practice with Data Changes

Changing your Variables' Data Types in Java

You can't. Once you've set your variable's data type, DO NOT assign a different data type to it. Otherwise, you'll get an error when you try to compile or run your code.

On the other hand, there are ways in Java that let you turn one data type into another. But even then, variables will still expect to have the same data types you've defined them to have.

Changing Data in Java

Just like our pseudocode, you can set and reset most of your variables using the Equals (=) sign.

Keeping Track of your Data

It's important. Very important. You'll see why in this example...

EXAMPLE:

(get your IDE ready...)

Let's say there's a square playground in a park within your neighbourhood. The playground is 20 feet long and wide.

You're babysitting your best friend's 5-year old son. Let's call him James. Kids in this playground has X-Y coordinates that tell you how far away they are from the Top-Left Corner of the playground (and there happens to be a bench that you're sitting in)

// James is a 5-year old kid.

// Kids have:

// - an X (sideways) Coordinate (Integer, between 0 and 20)

// - a Y (up-down) Coordinate (Integer, between 0 and 20)

```
class Kid{

int x;

int y;

}
```

James is running around the playground. Since you're babysitting, James is NOT allowed to set foot outside the playground.

You can't see James (because you're probably reading this instead) but you know what his X-Y coordinates are. Therefore,either X or Y coordinate cannot go below 0 or past 20.

First, let's initialize James as a Kid, then give him a location. He's at (12,3)

```
// James is a 5-year old kid with coordinates (12,3)

Kid James = new Kid();

James.x = 12;

James.y = 3;
```

And clearly, James is going to move around the playground randomly. In the past few seconds, James moved around like so:

-5 feet to left

-10 feet to right

-2 feet to up

-3 feet to right

-4 feet down

-12 feet left

-5 feet up

-2 feet down

-5 feet right

-3 feet up

-5 feet right

-2 feet down

-4 feet right

Question: Did James leave the playground? (did either X or Y go below 0 or above 20?)

Let's put James' movements on Java code. Before that, recall James' initial X-Y coordinates. We'll also comment James' current coordinates after his every move. Remember: moving left & up goes CLOSER to 0.

```java
// James is a 5-year old kid with coordinates (12,3)

Kid James = new Kid();

James.x = 12;

James.y = 3;

// 5 feet to left

James.x -= 5; // James is at (7,3)

// 10 feet to right

James.x += 10;// James is at (17,3)

// 2 feet to up
```

James.y -= 2;// James is at (17,1)

// 3 feet to right

James.x += 3;// James is at (20,1)

// 4 feet down

James.y += 4; // James is at (20,5)

// 12 feet left

James.x -= 12;// James is at (8,1)

// 5 feet up

James.y -= 5;// James is at (8,-4): James is outside the Playground!!!

// 2 feet down

James.y += 2; // James is at (8,-2): James is still outside the Playground!!!

// 5 feet right

James.x += 5; // James is at (13,-2): James is still outside the Playground!!!

// 3 feet up

James.y -= 3; // James is at (13,-5): James is still outside the Playground!!!

// 5 feet right

James.x += 5; // James is at (18,-5): James is still outside the Playground!!!

// 2 feet down

James.y += 2; // James is at (18,-3): James is still outside the Playground!!!

// 4 feet right

James.x += 4; // James is at (22,-3): James is still outside the Playground!!!

So James has been outside the playground for quite a long time. He just ran past the closest edge and past your bench. If you were babysitting James, you'd be in big trouble...

In cases where you set clear boundaries for your data, yet you have some code that sets your data to go past those boundaries (and nothing is done about it), it might create problems for your code later on.

Now you understand how crucial it is to keep track of your data. There are many aspects of coding that depend on it, such as Debugging and making sure your code works the way you intend it to.

On another example, if you designed a video game and your characters go out of bounds,your video game wouldn't be as good, won't it?

JAVA Workshop for Chapter 4

Go to an IDE of your choice. You may also use online IDE's such as rextester.com, ideone.com, or www.codechef.com/ide. (if you do, make sure to set your Programming Language to Java).

Chapter 5: Defining & Designing Functions

Now we'll move on to the parts of programming where the magic happens.

Functions.

Where data structures are used to represent "things" in this universe, you define functions as the "actions" or verbs in this universe. And you can make your functions do whatever you want/need it to do, as long as you know what you're doing. You can calculate math, write sentences for you, change or update data, sort out lists with tens of thousands of items, make websites for you, whatever you like. In reality, the possibilities can be endless.

But first let's understand the core parts of function design: its inputs, its output, its signature, its effects, and its functionality. Remember when we declared our Composite data? We first started figuring out the name of our whole data structure, then we started designing the data it consisted of. For designing and creating function code, the process is similar.

We define what the function does, including its inputs and outputs, then we implement its code so it does what we want it to do.

A Function's Inputs

You can set your function to accept whatever data you need it to.

These are called a function's arguments or parameters. Your function will use thisincoming data to perform what you intend it to.

Or, on the other hand, you can also have a function NOT require any inputs. Your function will then perform what you've programmed it to, but it won't need any incoming data.

A Function's Output

Your function can also return a data value - based on whatever you want to set it to. You can then program your function to output that same data type.

Or, you can also have a function NOT return anything. You can then program your function to do what you intend it to do, but it won't return any data after it executes.

In most programming languages, functions only return ONE thing - whether it be a data value, an entire list, compound data, or more.

However, you must make sure your function outputs whatever you have set it to. Say, if you want your function to output a String, the very last line of that function MUST return a String data type. If you set your function to have no outputs, your function MUST NOT return any data types after it executes.

Defining what your Function will Do

Now we figure out what EFFECT our function will have once we run it.

This is your function's main purpose - it's the reason why you're going to write these lines of code! Your function's effect will be whatever you intend it to do. Change data, create new data, calculate a few values together, whatever you want.

But isn't an Output and Effect the same thing? Well, no.

There is a difference between a function's OUTPUT and EFFECT. A function's output is the data it returns, while a function's effect is anything that the function does or any part of the program that the function's action has affected.

Key Function Rule-of-Thumb:

Make sure your function only does the only one thing you want it to do. A function that does too many things will not only complicate your code and make it look bad, but it will cause headaches and frustration for programming teammates.

However, your function can include and call on many other functions to help process something. These are called Helper Functions (we'll cover this later!)

A Function's Signature

Here is when we start writing our function's lines of code.

In most programming languages, a function's signature defines a function's name, inputs, outputs, and even particular traits it has.

We know what the function does, what it requires and what it returns. So we just need to start creating our function in our code by writing its signature - a line of code that declares the function's existence in the program. The signature will almost always include the name of the function, as well as any input data it may have.

Overall, function signatures from plenty of programming languages will generally look like this:

functionName(any inputs)

Implementing your Function

This can be the tricky part (unless you know exactly what you're doing)

In designing functions, the last thing you do is code your function's actual functionality. You would now know what inputs & outputs it has, as well as what it's trying to do. At first, you've essentially planned what your function will do.

Now you'll have your function actually do what you planned it to.

In most programming languages, you program the functionality in the next few lines after your function's signature.

Now let's practice designing and creating our functions.

JAVA-5a: Practice Defining Functions

Given what we've learned about functions so far, we can put it all into practice and start creating some.

A Function's Inputs

For practice, let's use comments to declare what inputs we want our function to have. Let's say we want a name (a string) as an input

// INPUT: - a name (String)

A Function's Output

Let's also use comments to declare what outputs we want our function to have. We'll continue designing our function. We now have an input, now we want to have an output.

// INPUT: - a name (String)

// OUTPUT: - an ID (Number)

Defining what your Function will Do

We'll continue designing our function. We now have an input and output. Now we figure out what it does when we run it.

Let's say we want it to come up with a random number per given name. We first write what we intend it to do, as comments:

// INPUT: - a name (String)

// OUTPUT: - an ID (Number)

// EFFECT: generates a random number for a given name

And there we go. Now we can start coding and creating the function.

JAVA-05b: Function Structure

Functions in JAVA

Overall, the syntax structure for Java functions is below:

<output's data type> functionName(<input data type> input1Name) {

// any code here,

return <data or variable with output's data type>;

}

Now let's look at the two main parts of the function code - the Signature and the Procedure body.

A Function's Signature

Similar to other programming languages, Java functions require what data types will be inputs and outputs.You will have to define your data inputs and outputs in your Java Function signature, which follows the format below:

<output's data type> functionName(<input data type> input1Name)

Note: if your Java functions don't have an output, the output type is 'void'.

Examples:

// INPUT: String

// OUTPUT: None

void f1(String input1)

// INPUT: None

// OUTPUT: Integer

int f2()

A Function's Procedure Body

This contains the actual code that the function will process.

In Java, the function procedure is placed within curly brackets - '{' and '}' - just after the signature.

Your function also needs to return the same data type that you've defined in the signature.

Preferably, the last (or only) line of your function body should be 'return <data with same type>'. For example, if your function outputs an integer, the last line should return some integer.

Below are expanded versions of previous examples:

```java
// INPUT: String

// OUTPUT: None

void f1(String input1) {

// body code

// no data output

}

// INPUT: None

// OUTPUT: Integer

int f2() {

// body code

return 12345

}
```

Special Notes on Java Functions

Here are a few key notes in Java functions:

-Since Java is purely Object-Oriented Programming, Functions in Java are mainly called Methods. They belong within classes and they describe behaviors that the class does.

-You place your function code within the curly brackets of your function.

-If your Java function returns data,you put the word 'return', then a variable name or some data value you want to return. Once the function reaches the 'return' line, it will output whatever data you've set it to, then the function will finish running.

-If your Java function returns nothing (the output value is called "void") you don't have to put a return line.

Function Example

Here's what the createID() function looks like in Java. We'll also consider numbers as data type Double:

// INPUT: - a name (String)

// OUTPUT: - an ID (Number)

```java
// EFFECT: generates a random number for a
given name

double createID(String input){

return rand();

}
```

Matching Data with Functions

Here's an inevitable truth when it comes to functions: they will almost always involve data in some way way.

Later on, you'll find that all sorts of different data structures will have at least one key procedure associated with it - either as a simple function or a complex algorithm.

Also, some data structures, by default, will have associated go-to function templates to use in programming. Remember this well; if you're given a certain data structure to work with, you should already have the function structure you'll need in mind.

JAVA-05c:Matching Data to Functions, Pt.1

Functions using Basic Data Types

There's usually no structure or template involved when dealing with Atomic Data. Functions may have atomic data as either inputs or outputs whenever necessary.

Let's recall the function examples from earlier. Note how they use basic data types, such as strings, integers, and booleans, as inputs and outputs to the function.

```
// INPUT: String

// OUTPUT: None

void f1(String input1) {

// body code

// no data output

}

// INPUT: None

// OUTPUT: Integer

int f2(){
```

// body code

return 12345;

}

Also, Functions can even modify existing global variables.

// Player1 Score, as an Integer

int score = 0;

// INPUT: - none

// OUTPUT: - none

// EFFECT: increments the score by one

void score1() { Score += 1}

Functions using Composite Data

The key thing to remember here is that there is an associated template function that accesses and deals with at least one component from the composite data (regardless of what data type each component is).

Also, each component will be treated as whatever data type it is; a String treated as a String, composite data as composite data, and so on.

We demonstrate this in code:

```
// Compound Data Structure of a Book:

// (either Class or Struct will do)

class Book {

String author;

String title;

int pagecount;

}

// TEMPLATE function:

// INPUT: - a Book

// OUTPUT: - none

// EFFECT: ?????

void bookTemplateFunc(Book b) {
```

```
//do something with one or all of:

// - b.author

// - b.title

// - b.pagecount

}
```

Here's an example of a printing function, based on the above template:

```
// INPUT: - a Book

// OUTPUT: - none

// EFFECT: prints book details

void printDetails(Book b) {

System.out.println(b.author) ;

System.out.println(b.title) ;

System.out.println(b.pagecount);

}
```

Methods: Functions for Object-Oriented Programming

In Object-oriented programming, data and procedures are bundled in data structures called classes.

Functions are called Methods and class variables are called Fields.

You can think of Methods within a class as 'behaviours' - or what actions an instance of that class can do.

To describe Class Methods in comments, simply document the behaviours a class object can do. For example:

// A Space Invaders Tank can:

// -move left

// - move right

// - shoot a missile

// A Dog can:

// - walk

// - bark

// - sit

// - eat

Afterwards, each behaviour or action can be implemented as a class method.

// A Space Invaders Tank can:

// -move left

// - move right

// - shoot a missile

```
class Tank {

void moveLeft() {

// some procedure code

}

void moveRight() {

// some procedure code

}

void shootMissile() {
```

```
// some procedure code
  }
}

// A Dog can:
// - walk
// - bark
// - sit
// - eat
class Dog {
void walk(direction: String) {
// some procedure code
}
void bark() {
// some procedure code
}
void sit() {
```

```
// some procedure code

}

void eat() {

// some procedure code

}

}
```

So far, we've only been working with functions and data we're familiar with. Once we start encountering more complex data structures, you'll find that they're all still associated with certain function procedures.

JAVA Workshop for Chapter 5

Designing & Calling Functions

First, go to an IDE of your choice. Online IDE's include Rextester (rextester.com), CodeChef (www.codechef.com/ide), and Ideone (https://ideone.com/).

On your Main Function, replace ALL code within it, then copy-paste all the code within the dotted lines below.Make sure it's between the curly brackets of the main() function.

```
public static void main(String args[]) {

// - - - -- - - - -- - - - -- - - - -- - - - -

class calculator{

// INPUT: - two Integers

// OUTPUT: - a result(Integer)

// EFFECT: add two integers together & give result
```

Chapter 6: Intro To Designing Worlds & Simple Apps, Pt1

At this point, you know how to interpret real-life objects as computer data representations, as well as interpreting actions & procedures as programming functions.

Now, you'll begin the design process. You start to describe virtual worlds and apps, almost always visually. You prepare to translate your ideas into code and data.

Just as if you were a carpenter thinking of how to build your house, you use the same approach towards developing apps and game worlds. You identify all the components required to build your project.

Simple App Design Process

There are three key things about your idea that you need to identify: the facts behind your idea, what remains constant, and what will change/vary.

The reason for this is to give you and other programmers as much control and stability over your data as possible. You would know what type of data you would be working with and if/how that data would or would not change. Experienced programmers can then check if a particular data structure or function is designed the way it was intended to be.

To guide you through this process, we'll describe the classic Snake game - and identify plenty of details about the game from a programmer's standpoint. It will be as if we're designing the game for the first time. As if we're in the 70's.

Identifying the FACTS

First, you need the facts. You need to describe what your idea is about, what's involved, etc. Describe as much detail as you can, including the environment and key figures you provide.

Example:

In a single game of Snake, there exists a snake with a head and body, as well as food items that appear randomly. The snake's head, all segments

of its body, and the food pieces have an X-Y coordinate and a visual representation (since they have similar traits, they can be grouped together as a game sprite). An X-Y coordinate represents a location within the playable zone: a rectangular area with a height and width. A score keeps track of how many food items have been eaten.

The player changes which direction the snake will travel to: up, down, left, and right. The game ends when the snake either hits a wall or runs into one of its body segments.

The snake grows by one body segment after the snake head "eats a food item" (appears on the same coordinate as a food item).

[food] + [head] [body] [body]

=

[head] [body] [body] [body]

Identifying what's CONSTANT

Second, you need to identify what elements in your world or app remain consistent throughout the programming. Also, identify what will exist in your idea unconditionally.

Example:

The food items, snake head, and body segments have consistent images.

The playing board has a fixed width and height.

Identifying what CHANGES/VARIES

Third, identify what will change or vary when the program runs.

Example:

The food items, snake head, and body segments all have varying X-Y coordinates throughout the game. The number of body segments vary, from the initial number of 2, all the way to as much as possible.

Turning your ideas into code

Now, you take note of all the facts, descriptions, and ideas you've come up with. You'll be making data representations of them.

Early in the book, there is a great reason why we've used comments to describe all the information we are going to create.It's because they help select the best possible data representation for each pint of information you have. And after you've described what your app or world will be about, you'll start developing that digital world first by using comments.

Example: For each fact and idea about the Snake game that we've come up with, we'll use general comments to hint how they should be represented by data.

 A Game Sprite has:

- an X-coordinate (Integer)

- a Y-coordinate (Integer)

- an image to represent itself (choose your visual representation)

Snake Heads, Snake Body Segments, and Food Pieces

are each represented by Game Sprites

An EntireSnake contains:

- a Snake Head (GameSprite)

- a list of Snake Body Segments (list of GameSprites)

A FullSnake can:

- eat food

- grow

- move on the board

The Playable Board has:

- a fixed length (Integer)

- a fixed width (Integer)

A Game of Snake has:

- a playable board (Playable Board Class)

- food items (list of Food)

- the Snake (EntireSnake)

- a Score Count (Integer)

A Game of Snake can:

- start a new game

- end the game (as a loss or win)

- update a game in progress

- update the score

- move the snake on keypresses

- create or delete food items

Notice how there is no actual code written yet; only comments.

The beauty of this process is that, given the facts and ideas (as well as their data representations), we can start creating the code in any language we want. We now know what will be data structures, classes, integers, and so on.

We do need to go over more tools, so we will continue with design later on.

Meanwhile, in the next big workshop, you will be converting idea comments into actual code. Good luck and have fun!

JAVA BIG Workshop A

Game Design: the Data & Functions

First, go to an IDE of your choice. Online IDE's include Rextester (rextester.com), CodeChef (www.codechef.com/ide), and Ideone (https://ideone.com/).

You're going to practice designing Data Structures and Functions - as if you were designing an app yourself.

All you'll be given is a set of comments describing the data objects within a very, very simple video game. If you can, you may continue developing it into a full-blown game.

Copy and paste all the comment code below, then start writing code for the data definitions.

As you improve your programming and learn more tricks over time, you can revisit this workshop and re-create it using your new skills.

For example: for the functions and class methods, they might need more intermediate functionality. So you can come back to them later - after going through the necessary chapters.

If you feel like you want to create or remove new Fields, Classes, or Methods, feel free to do so.

Now, let's move forward.

The game we'll be designing is...

PONG!

Good luck!

// - - - - -- - - - - -- - - - - -- - - -- - - - - -

// A Game Sprite Class has:

// - a Width (Integer)

// - a Height (Integer)

// - an X-coordinate (Integer)

// - a Y-coordinate (Integer)

// A Ball Class has:

// - all properties of a Game Sprite

// - either an UP or DOWN direction (String)

// - either a LEFT or RIGHT direction (String)

// A Ball Class can:

// - move in all 4 diagonal directions

Chapter 7: Boolean Logic And Operators

For every line or expression that needs to return a Boolean, use these operators to compare values together.

It's best to compare Atomic Data Types, such as Strings, Integers, Numbers and even Booleans themselves. Remember: Some programming languages are more strict about what data types you use as values; and some are more lax.

You can also compare Function and Method outputs, as we'll show later, but you have to make sure that they return the exact data types that you'll be comparing.

Boolean Logic is particularly important for managing more sophisticated algorithms, functions, and methods - so take note.

Basic Boolean Logic:

The three basic Boolean Operators are AND, OR, and NOT. Use these to compare booleans together.

Speaking of comparing booleans, if you compare booleans together using the boolean operators from above, you'll get a result based on the below:

The AND operator:

Using the AND operator, comparing two values together will return TRUE - if, and only if, both values are true.

TRUE and TRUE returns TRUE

TRUE and FALSE returns FALSE

FALSE and TRUE returns FALSE

FALSE and FALSE returns FALSE

The OR operator:

Comparing two values together using the OR operator will return TRUE - if at least one value is true.

TRUE or TRUE returns TRUE

TRUE or FALSE returns TRUE

FALSE or TRUE returns TRUE

FALSE or FALSE returns FALSE

Multiple Boolean Operators:

You can also compare multiple boolean values together. But to keep things simple (and not mess up your code), make sure you're only comparing with either the AND or OR operator - but not both.

(TRUE and FALSE and FALSE and TRUE) returns FALSE

(TRUE or FALSE or TRUE or FALSE) returns TRUE

The NOT operator:

You can convert a single Boolean into its opposite value using the NOT operator.

not TRUE returns FALSE

not FALSE returns TRUE

Function Outputs and Variables

You can compare these values using Boolean Operators with Functions that return a Boolean as a data type.

Here's an example in Pseudocode:

INPUT: - two integers

OUTPUT: - Boolean

EFFECT: check if integer a is larger than integer b

check(a, b) {

return a > b

}

If implemented in real code, the pseudocode below should print true,

print check(12, 1) AND check(100, 1)

You can also compare variables that hold booleans. In most languages, they can be any variable type.

Here's an example in Pseudocode:

Two Global Variables that hold Booleans:

YOUARECOOL = true

YOUAREAWESOME = true

If implemented in real code, the pseudocode below would also print true,

print YOUARECOOL OR YOUAREAWESOME

Fundamental Programming Operators

These operators are designed to either manipulate your data or compare/contrast two values together.

These operators are frequently used to develop functionality in a lot of code - from complex algorithms to simple functions. Programmers will almost always use these operators well.

An important note here is to use these operators with a purpose. The point behind leaving comments to describe your code does just that. If you - or your colleague - were trying to compare two values together, you would use comments to describe what's required. Afterwards, whoever is writing the actual code can add the right functionality to your code.

Again, it's best to compare Atomic Data Types, such as Strings, Integers, Numbers and even Booleans themselves.

Just like the Boolean Operators, you can compare Function and Method outputs, but you have to make sure that they return the exact data types that you'll be comparing.

The General Assignment operator:

This is simply using the Equals Sign (=) to assign data.

Yes, you must have been using this the whole time! We just wanted to keep things simple and add steps one at a time.

Just to be sure, it was set up like this:

(1st Variable Name) = (Value or expression to change 1st Variable Value to);

Comparison operators:

These are what you use to compare a value greater than/ less than /or equal toanother value.

In most languages, you can use these to compare Integers and Numbers. So either variables with those data types or functions/methods that return those types.

Greater Than: (your data) > (other data)

Greater Than or Equal to: (your data) >= (other data)

Less Than: (your data) < (other data)

Less Than or equal to: (your data) < (other data)

Equality operators:

Use these operators between to values to compare whether or not two values are equal to each other.

Is Equal To: (value1) == (value2)

Is NOT Equal To: (value1) != (value2)

In most languages, the '==' and '!=' will be consistently compare two values for equality.

Mathematic Assignment operators:

These are similar to the general assignment operator (a single equals sign, '='; the same operator you set your variables!). However, in most languages, you can modify the left-hand variable using the right-hand-value, depending on what your Assignment Operator is.

Essentially, the operator will be an Equals Sign, just like the assignment operator, with an additional character before it. this additional character will determine what value your Assignment Operator is.

Essentially, the code will look something like this:

(1st Variable) (Assignment Operator) (Value to change 1st Variable with)

General Pseudocode examples:

Set x to 12:

x = 12

Add 8:

x += 8

Subtract 10:

x -= 10

Multiply by 10:

x *= 10

Divide by 20:

x /= 10

In most programming languages, these assignment operators will be consistent throughout:

Add to the 1st Value: (1st Value) += (Value to Add)

Multiply the 1st Value: (1st Value) *= (Value to Multiply)

Divide the 1st Value: (1st Value) /= (Value to Divide)

Modulus to the 1st Value: (1st Value) %= (Value to Divide, without Remainders)

For obvious reasons, these are best used with numerical data types - such as Integers and Numbers. Of course, we need numbers to do math with!

JAVA-07: Operators in Java

Logic Operators.

In Java, the Three Basic Logic Operators are so:

AND operator: &&

OR operator: ||

NOT operator: !(just a single exclamation mark)

Here's a few examples in Java Code:

```java
// Prints False:

if (true && false) {

System.out.println("True");

}

else System.out.println("False");

// Prints False:

if (true || false) { System.out.println("True")
;};

// Prints False:

if (!true) { System.out.println("True") ;}

else System.out.println("False");
```

Chapter 8: Conditional Statements, If & Else

Among all programming languages, the concept of IF & Else statements is quite simple: a few lines of code will either execute or not, depending on certain conditions.

Importance

IF/ELSE statements will be one of the most frequently used code in programming. As a matter of fact. more advanced code will depend on these statements often.

Analysis

In general code comments, here is a sample IF-ELSE statement:

EFFECT: check condition A

- run True Procedure on TRUE

- run False Procedure on FALSE

Now, let's analyze the parts of the code above.

Documentation

As always, it's best practice to describe your code's functionality before creating it.

If you recall Programming Functions from a previous chapter, functions have a certain effect you intend it to perform once it has been called.

IF/ELSE statements are also meant to create an effect (given the condition holds true) in either your functions or executable code.

In our documentation, we describe our IF/ELSE statement with the conditions we look for and the effects we want to occur.

EFFECT: check condition A

- run True Procedure on TRUE

- run False Procedure on FALSE

Parts of the IF statement

In almost all programming languages, there are three parts to an IF statement. The first is the word 'if'; here, your code declares an IF statement. The second and third are the Condition and the Executable Code.

if Condition {

Executable code

}

Condition

In an IF-Statement, the expression just after the IF is the condition. Thecode in the condition must return a boolean - either TRUE or FALSE. Here, you can use fields that contain booleans, compare two values usingcomparison operators (==, !=, >, <, and more), or even use boolean operators on two values (AND, NOT, OR)

if conditionA ==TRUE {

.....

}

Executable Code

When the condition expression returns true, the program will run the executable code - all the code after the condition until its

But inthe condition returns false, the program will skip the executable code and move on.

if conditionA ==TRUE runFunctionA()

For multiple lines of executable code, we'll place them within curly brackets "{ }". Since we only use pseudocode, for now, you may not necessarily have to use curly brackets. You do have to communicate where the executable code ends though.

if conditionB ==TRUE {

runFunctionB()

runFunctionC()

}

Here's an alternate example of executable code.

if conditionB ==TRUE,

runFunctionB()

runFunctionC()

endif

ELSE Statement

After the condition returns false, the program will skip over the Executable Code. But if you have an ELSE statement, the program will instead run the executable code following that ELSE statement.

Again, multiple lines of executable code are also placed within curly brackets "{ }". Otherwise, you may communicate your pseudocode whichever way you'd like (just as long as you indicate where the executable code ends).

```
if conditionB ==TRUE {

runFunctionB()

runFunctionC()

}
```

else {

runFunctionD()

runFunctionE()

}

Applying IF-ELSE Statements

Most programming languages will have conditionals in the following format: Type -> Condition -> Executable Code. The type of conditional statement can be IF, ELSE, or many other types available on any given programming language.

JAVA-08: IF,ELSE Statements

Now let's create IF-ELSE statements in real code.

Take note of the three parts of a conditional statement: the type, condition, and executable code. We'll create all three parts in Java.

Documentation:

Before we first start to write code, it's important to understand and describe what our procedure will be. Therefore, we use comments to document our procedures.

Below is the documentation for the pseudocode from the previous chapter:

// EFFECT: check condition A

// - run True Procedure if TRUE

// - run False Procedure if FALSE

Again, it's important to get into the habit of documenting your code procedure and data structures. This will come in handy with programming teams, as well as 3rd-party programmers that want to reference your code.

There doesn't have to be a clear method on how to document your code; it just have to be easily understandable.

Below is the implementation based on the documentation above, in Java code:

```java
if (conditionA == true) {

trueProcedure();

}

else {

falseProcedure();

}
```

Next, we'll go over the format for all three parts of the conditional statement

Conditional Type

This is simple. It's just the words 'if', 'else', or any other conditional type in Java.

```java
if (...)...

else ...
```

Condition

In Java, you place the condition code within parentheses "( )". Just remember: the code in the condition part must return a boolean. The boolean operators, comparisons, and other expressions from the Previous section will come in handy for the condition.

For 'else', it requires no condition statement. When the condition from the corresponding 'if' statement produces false, the 'else' executive code will be run.

if (conditionA ==true) ...

else ...

Executable Code

In Java, the executable code can be any procedural code just after the condition part.

For multiple lines of executable code, it's just like our pseudocode example. We place them within curly brackets "{ }".

Chapter 9: Helper Functions

The concept behind helper functions is quite simple.

A larger, complex, general function will call other smaller, more specialized functions to achieve its given purpose.

And to do this, you must remember one important thing...

A Key Concept: The Small Parts of the Whole

If it's one thing you need to learn about programming that encompasses EVERY single aspect of programming, it's this one phrase:

"Break down a large concept into several smaller parts, then again into even smaller parts, until you have the very basic elements. Define and create what each of those basic elements are, then continue building your concept piece by piece until it's finished."

For example, if you've read up to the chapter where you've designed the Snake Game, you've noticed that creating an app follows the above: break down the large app into several data structures, which then are further broken down into either other Data Structures or atomic data types.

In this chapter, we'll apply this large-to-small concept towards Functions and Class Methods.

And the best way to explore the Helper Function concept is to see it in action.

Example: Robotic Legs

Take a look at this method for the class Droid, in Pseudocode. Assume that it's part of a larger, working, artificial intelligence program for the Droid:

INPUT: - none

OUTPUT: - none

EFFECT: Droid walks forward across terrain, using its feet, unless there is something the droid cannot walk over.

walk() {

(checking for obstacles in the front)

(return if droid cannot walk over obstacle)

if frontSensor detectsObject

& height of objectDetected > 1/2 of Droid.height

& distance of objectDetected <= 1Ft) {

return

}

(check if left foot is currently behind right foot)

(make a left foot step if so)

if (rightFoot y-coordinate > leftFoot y-coordinate) {

- transferBalance to rightFoot

- lift leftLeg

- use rightFoot to moveBalanceForward

- move leftFoot Forward, PastOtherFoot

- place leftFoot On the Ground

}

(check if right foot is currently behind left foot)

(make a right foot step if so)

if (leftFoot y-coordinate > rightFoot y-coordinate) {

- transferBalance to leftFoot

- lift rightLeg

- use leftFoot to moveBalanceForward

- move rightFoot Forward, PastOtherFoot

- place rightFoot On the Ground

}

}

Let's assume that this pseudocode is fully functional and there really are no coding errors with this code.

However, the class method walk() is far too long and not quite pleasant to look at. For a single method,it does far too many things. If a single error were to occur on this code, the debugging process would be extremely difficult. The programmer would have to review every single phrase of code to figure out what's wrong.

But hey, At least the walk() method already uses helper functions on some of its lines. The code could be worse. Instead of the code above, what if a majority of the lines within the walk() method moved every single droid-muscle required, in every angle necessary, and moved every single leg part to the space it's supposed to be in? That would be a lot of lines...

Remember when we mentioned "breaking down large concepts into smaller parts?" Let's do it for the walk() method. We're going to see how many related lines of code can we condense into smaller methods.

This practice will be in pseudocode, to help you understand this process beyond any one programming language in particular.

The Helper Functions

The first helper function we can make is this IF statement:

if frontSensor detectsObject

& height of objectDetected > 1/2 of Droid.height

& distance of objectDetected <= 1Ft) {

That is quite a handful for just the conditional portion. What if we can simplify it into a Helper Function? We know that the entire conditional takes no inputs and outputs a boolean. Here, we're going to take the entire conditional part and have it as a function on its own:

INPUT: - none

OUTPUT: - boolean

EFFECT: returns TRUE if Droid detects an obstacle it cannot walk over

checkObstacle() {

return true if frontSensor detectsObject

& height of objectDetected > 1/2 of Droid.height

& distance of objectDetected <= 1Ft)

}

Then, the IF-statement turns into this simple line of code:

if checkObstacle() is true,return

Next, remember the two stepping portions? They were quite lengthy, weren't they?

But what if we turned them both into Helper Functions? They would have distinct, focused functionality. Also, they would look cleaner and more simple.Here, we will name them leftFootStep() and rightFootStep(), respectively:

INPUT: - none

OUTPUT: - none

EFFECT: check if left foot is currently behind right foot,

then make a left foot step if so

leftFootStep() {

if rightFoot y-coordinate > leftFoot y-coordinate {

- transferBalance to rightFoot

- lift leftLeg

- use rightFoot to moveBalanceForward

- move leftFoot Forward, PastOtherFoot

- place leftFoot On the Ground

}

}

INPUT: - none

OUTPUT: - none

EFFECT: check if right foot is currently behind left foot,

then make a right foot step if so

void rightFootStep() {

if leftFoot y-coordinate > rightFoot y-coordinate {

- transferBalance to leftFoot

- lift rightLeg

- use leftFoot to moveBalanceForward

- move rightFoot Forward, PastOtherFoot

- place rightFoot On the Ground

}

}

The Larger Function

After converting significant portions of code into helper functions, the walk() method now calls each helper function where necessary. All functions now have a single purpose.

```
// INPUT: - none

// OUTPUT: - none

// EFFECT: Droid walks forward across terrain

void walk() {

if (checkObstacle()) return

leftFootStep()

rightFootStep()

}
```

Do you notice how much cleaner and simple the method walk() is now?

And if you had to debug something, it would be much more simple. If there's an error in the programming about checking obstacles or stepping with either foot, you can focus on that specific helper function and any code inside it.

Putting it All Together

The concept behind helper functions is simple: for a bigger, general function, give it a general purpose, then have it call other smaller single-purpose functions to help achieve its purpose.

As mentioned earlier, this philosophy applies to all programming languages.

Chapter 10: Local Variables

The Function, and Its Locals

You can define variables within a function/method to hold key data for that function/method to use.

These are called Local Variables, or locals for short.

Later on, you will need locals for more advanced concepts, such as accumulator variables and even within algorithms.

Local Variables V.S. Global Variables

Here are the key differences between Local and Global variables.

Global variables exist throughout your entire code file. They can generally be accessed anywhere in your code.

Local Variables can only be accessed within the functions/methodsthat they're defined in.

Defining Locals

In most programming languages, you would simply define a local variable as if you were defining a global one. The difference is that you define the local variable within the function code only.

Here is a pseudocode example where we define local variables, as opposed to global variables:

Chapter 11: Frontend Vs. Backend Vs. Full-Stack Developers

Before we dive into backend development, it's worth diverting to understand the difference between the three types of developers involved in web development – backend, frontend, and full-stack.

Right now, there are over 1.5 billion websites on the internet, and that number is continuously rising. The people responsible for coding and building those websites, not to mention analyzing and maintaining them, are the web developers.

Websites are critical in any company's bid to be competitive in a tough market.And that means the number of jobs for web developers is also on the rise. But how do you determine which type of web development work you want to do? Here, we break down the three main types of web app developers.

Frontend Development

A website's frontend is the bit users see and interact with. Whatever you see when you navigate the internet, including colors, fonts, sliders, dropdown menus, and more, are all controlled by your browser.

Tools and Skills

A frontend developer is responsible for the user-facing code and immersive infrastructure of a website. To fulfill their objectives, they must be proficient in CSS, HTML, and JavaScript. They also need familiarity with certain frameworks, such as Backbone, Foundation, Bootstrap, EmberJS, and AngularJS. All of these are used to ensure the content looks great, regardless of platform or device. Frontend developers must also be familiar with libraries that package the code into a useful time-saving form, such as LESS and jquery.

Many job descriptions for frontend developers also request some Ajax experience, a technique that downloads server data in the background so pages can load dynamically.

These tools allow frontend developers to work with user-experience analysts or designers to take a wireframe or mockup from the development stage to delivery. A good frontend developer can identify user-experience issues accurately, providing code solutions and recommendations as appropriate. They must also be able to work fluidly with other business teams to understand opportunities, goals, and needs, executing the right solutions at the right time.

While a frontend developer has significant responsibility, the job is rewarding. One way to describe the involvement of a frontend developer is to say that it is their job to design the interior of a house a backend developer built, and the homeowner gets to dictate the décor.In reality, frontend developers often get more excited about their work because they get to let their creative sides take over.

Open any website on your computer. Everything you see is the result of a frontend developer's hard work. A designer may have done the graphics and logo. A photographer or a stock-photo website supplied the pictures, and a copywriter wrote the text. But all that was put together by a frontend developer, translated into something web-compatible, and given to you in an interactive format you can understand.

Backend Development

All that frontend stuff is great, but what makes it all happen? Where does all the data get stored? That's where the backend steps in. A website's backend comprises three things – server, application, database. The developer is responsible for building the technology powering all three components, maintaining it so that the website's frontend can exist, the bit the user sees.

Tools and Skills

To make all three components talk to one another, a backend developer uses a server-side language to build the application. They then use tools to find data, save it, change it, code it, and serve it back to the user. Server-side languages include Java, PHP, .Net, Python, and Ruby, while the data tools include Oracle, MySQL, and SQL Server.

Job descriptions for backend developers often ask for prior experience using the following:

- PHP frameworks, such as CakePHP, Symfony, and Zend

- VCS (version control software) such as CVS, SVN, and Git

- Linux to develop and deploy applications.

Backend developers use tools like these to create web applications or contribute to existing ones, writing portable, clean, documented code. Before they can write that code, they must get together with business stakeholders to ensure they know their needs. Those needs must then be translated into technical requirements and build the most effective solution to build the required technology.

Backend development is all about data manipulation, trading data between connected systems, websites, and devices, and creating useful APIs the public can use.

Go back to that website you opened in the section on frontend development. When you open it, information is sent to your mobile or desktop device by a server. That information becomes the page you are looking at. If you provide a website with personal information, such as login details, it is stored and automatically called up when you go back to the site — that is also down to a backend developer.

Full-Stack Development

Often, the distinction between front and backend development is not black and white. Frontend developers sometimes need to learn backend skills, while backend developers often need to know how to do some frontend work. All developers need a certain amount of cross-discipline and must, in many cases, be generalists.

That is where the full0stack developer comes in. A jack of all trades, the full-stack role became popular several years ago, thanks to the engineering department at Facebook. The idea behind the role is to work across the full technology stack – the front and backend.

When you can work professionally on the client and server side, more doors are open to you, but it is by no means an easy job. To use cooking as an analogy, you can be a good baker or a good cook, but doing both equally well requires experience and time. It's not about following a recipe in front of you – it's about having the right ingredients to create something truly marvelous.

Tools and Skills

Like a backend developer, a full-stack developer works mostly on the server side but is also fluent in the frontend language. That means they can control how a website's content looks to a user.

A full-stack developer needs to know the tools they can use, depending on their current client or project. They also need knowledge of how the web works on every level. That includes setting up the Linux servers and configuring them, writing the server-side APIs, understanding and writing JavaScript on the client-side to power applications, and using CSS to do the design work.

These tools allow a full-stack developer to identify both the server and client-side solution responsibilities and lay out the pros and cons of all the different solutions available.

Chapter 12: Setting Up Your Java Environment

Depending on what type of Java application you want to develop, you have a choice of three SDKs – Software Development Kits:

- Java SE (Standard Edition) – this SDK is primarily used to develop desktop applications and is also known as JDK (Java Development Kit).

- Java ME (Mobile Edition) – this SDK is primarily used to develop mobile applications and applications for TV-oriented devices. You must install JDK before you can use this one.

- Java EE (Enterprise Edition) – this SDK is primarily used to develop component-based enterprise apps, for example, Java servlet, Enterprise JavaBean, and JSP. It also requires JDK to be installed first.

We are going to focus on the first one, Java SE or JDK.

Installing JDK on Windows

Step One

The first step is to uninstall older JDK versions you may have on your machine. Although you can run more than one version, it does get messy.

- Open your Control Panel and click on Programs>Programs and Features

- Click on Add/Remove Programs

- Now uninstall everything starting with Java – Java SE Runtime, Java X Update, and so on.

Step Two

Now we can download a fresh install of the JDK

-   Open https://www.oracle.com/java/technologies/javase-jdk16-downloads.html

- Click on Oracle JDK

- Click on JDK Download

- Download the latest version of the Windows x64 Installer – make sure to accept the license agreement, or you cannot go any further

Step Three

Now we need to install JDK

- Find the installer and double-click on it to run it

- If you are asked to provide system permission, click on Yes. This will allow the installer to self-execute, and the Installer Welcome Screen will appear on your monitor

- Click on Next, and the installation process can begin

- The next screen will show you some options for changing the installation path. Keep the default or change to a different one as you wish – either way, note down where JDK is being installed

- Click on Next, and the installation will begin – a progress screen will be shown

Step Four

Now you need to check the installation has been successful:

- Open your command prompt – right-click on your start menu and click on Command Prompt. Alternatively, just type Command Prompt into the search bar and click the result

- When your command window opens, type the following command at the prompt:

java -version

You should see something like the image below on your screen:

If you see a message saying, "- java is not recognized," or an older version is shown – a previous one you installed – we need to take an additional step. To use the JDK version you installed, you may need to set the environment variable – details in the next step.

Step Five

These steps are ONLY required IF you see anything on your screen other than the correct JDK version.

Follow these steps to set the environment variable:

- Right-click your start bar

- Click on My Computer (This PC)

- Click on Properties

- Click on Advanced System Settings

These steps open your Windows Settings panel as you see below:

- Click on the button at the bottom that reads Environment Variables

- Click on the System Variables option and then click on Path

- Click on Edit

We can now input the path for the installed version of the JDK to the system path.

First – if the installer adds the path to the system path, delete it as you see in the image below:

- Delete the path relating to the previous JDK version

- If JAVA_HOME is set, update it

- Click on the New button

- Add the path to the JDK bin directory – it should be something likeC:\Java\Oracle\jdk-16\bin

- Click on the OK button three times, and all windows will close.

The JDK 16 is now set on the system's environment variables, allowing you to access it from the command console.

Step Six

Open the command console and check the Java version as you did earlier:

java -version

Step Seven

Now you need to download an IDE — Integrated Development Environment. We'll be using Eclipse:

- Open https://www.eclipse.org/downloads

- Click on Get Eclipse IDE and choose Download Packages

- Click on Eclipse IDE for Java Developers and Windows x86_64

Step Eight

Install the IDE:

- Find and unzip the downloaded file

- Save it to a directory — anywhere you want, just make a note of where it is

The zip version is best because you don't have to run an installer. And, when you don't need it anymore, you can simply delete the whole directory. Rename or move the directory as you wish, so long as you know where it is and what it's called.

Getting Started with Java on Windows

To get you used to working with Java, we'll start with the Hello World example. We will write the code, compile it, and execute it.

- Open the IDE and type in the following code. Save it as HelloWorld.java and close the Editor:

```
class HelloWorld {

public static void main( String[] args ) {

System.out.println( "Hello World !!\n" );

}

}
```

- Open your command prompt and go to the path where your Java program is saved. The commands below can be used to compile the program and execute it:

Compile - Specify the correct file name and extension

javac HelloWorld.java

Execute – Specify the correct file name

java HelloWorld

Output

Hello World !!

That is how easy it is to install Java on Windows and use it to write, compile and execute a program.

Installing JDK on macOS

STEP ONE

First, you need to see if JDK is already installed on your system – on some macOS computers, it comes pre-installed as standard:

- Open a Terminal on your computer – type "terminal" into the search bar or open Finder>Utilities>Terminal

- Once your Terminal is open, type in the following command:

javac -version

If you see a JDK version number on your screen, you already have JDK installed. If the JDK version number is below 16, you will need to upgrade to the latest version, which you can fund in the next step. You will also need to install the latest version if you see "Command not found" on your screen.

If you see a message that reads, "To open javac, you need a Java runtime" on your screen, choose Install and follow the directions to install the JDK.

STEP TWO

If your version needs updating or Java is not installed on your machine, you must follow these steps:

- Open https://www.oracle.com/java/technologies/javase-jdk16-downloads.html

- Click on Oracle JDK

- Click on JDK Download

- Click the macOS DMG Installer – it will look something like this - jdk-16.0.{x}_osx-x64_bin.dmg

STEP THREE

Now you can install the file:

- Find and double-click on the DMG file you downloaded

- Follow the directions on your screen to install it

- Eject the DMG file

STEP FOUR

To verify the installation, open a Terminal and type in these commands:

// Display the JDK version

javac -version

javac 16.0.{x}

```
// Display the JRE version

java -version

java version "16.0.{x}"

......

// Display the location of Java Compiler

which javac

/usr/bin/javac

// Display the location of Java Runtime

which java

/usr/bin/java
```

Getting Started with Java on macOS

As explained in the Windows tutorial, we can get used to working with Java by writing the HelloWorld program. You will need to install a text editor, such as Atom or Sublime Text, so go ahead and do this now – all instructions to install will be on the relevant website.

Next, you need to create a new directory:

- Open Finder>Go and click on Home

- Click on File>New Folder and name it myProject

In macOS, the user's home directory can be referenced as ~ so you can reference the new project as ~/myProject.

Open your text editor and input the code below. Name it Hello.java and save it under ~/myProject.

Chapter 13: Java With Spring

This chapter will look at initializing and developing a website backend using Spring. It will be covered in four separate parts:

- Choose your framework

- Initialize your Spring project

- Program the backend

- Build the backend

We'll break those down in a moment but, first, you need to install Spring. You can find all the relevant details at https://docs.spring.io/spring-boot/docs/current/reference/html/getting-started.html

Now let's look into the first two parts this tutorial comprises:

Choose your Framework

You can build a website in hundreds of different ways, using any one of multiple languages. There isn't a right or wrong way to do it, and you could even use the same framework for the back and frontend.We will use an easy framework that can be used on any project, even those that rapidly scale – Java with Spring.

Initializing Your Spring Project

Before we dive into this, we need to know what Spring is.

Spring is a user-friendly framework that allows for easy program decoupling. It uses dependency injection to make it easier to switch implementations or components – more about that in a while.

The main reason why Spring is so popular for the backend is that it offers plenty of ready-to-use components for web applications. For example, with Spring Security, you can have robust, easy access control, while Spring Data helps you easily connect to databases.

Then there is Spring Initializer, which we will use to initialize our project. If you haven't already, go ahead and download Spring onto your system, then open the Spring Assistant. Here, you will see several options, and you will need to choose the following:

- Your project

- The language

- The relevant Spring Boot version

- The project's metadata

- The dependencies.

Let's see what all these are:

Your Project

You will need to choose between Maven and Gradle – later, there will be a separate tutorial for both of these but, for now, we will use Gradle. Both are tools that help automate your application's build. We need to tell it what our project dependencies are, for example, Spring, and then it will build it.

The Language

As this book is about Java, that is what we will select.

The Relevant Spring Boot Version

Simply select the version you downloaded.

What is Spring Boot? Spring is used to program the application, while Spring Boot looks after the overheads in running the application. It will examine the application, make checks and assumptions, and ensure you have the standard configurations your application needs to run. For example, it has embedded server-functionalities, so you don't need to think about that. Gradle will then take it all and build your Java application.

The Project's Metadata

In this section, fields one and two detail the software owner and the name of the application. The most common way is to use the schema com.[organization name].[software name]. The more interesting options are the Java versions and packaging.

For the version, it should be the most stable, up-to-date release. We'll discuss packaging below.

The Packaging

When you build an application using Java, you can choose between two file types - .jar and .war. Typically, .war files are web app archives that run in the application's server. A .jar file is a Java Archive file, and this also runs in the application server and on a user's machine. We will use .jar.

The Dependencies

Here, you choose further dependencies you want to be defined, like Spring Data or Spring Security. For now, leave this blank. We will manually add the relevant dependencies when we need them.

Once you have done all that, go ahead and click on the Generate button to generate the new project.

Program the Backend

Our project is now initialized, and we can now get down to programming the Backend. That will take five steps:

- Organize the folder structure for your project

- Understand what has been generated

- Adding a single endpoint – so that you can understand it

- Adding a database connection so that data can be stored

- Adding simple authentication ensuring private endpoints.

Let's get started.

Organizing the folder structure

We will use the folder structure below for this project:

- The project folder

- The backend

- The frontend

Move the folder your Spring Initializer generated into the project folder. Rename it to Backend.

Understand what has been generated

Open the project in your Java IDE and make sure you install Gradle. We installed Eclipse, so follow these steps to install the Gradle Eclipse plugin:

1. Open Eclipse and click the Help menu

2. Choose Eclipse Marketplace

3. Type Gradle into the search bar

4. Click the Install button

5. Accept the license and click on Finish

When you have done this, Eclipse will restart.

Right now, because there is nothing in your project, running it will result in it terminating straight away as it doesn't have anything to do.

Before we do anything else, we need to look at what was generated and what it all means.

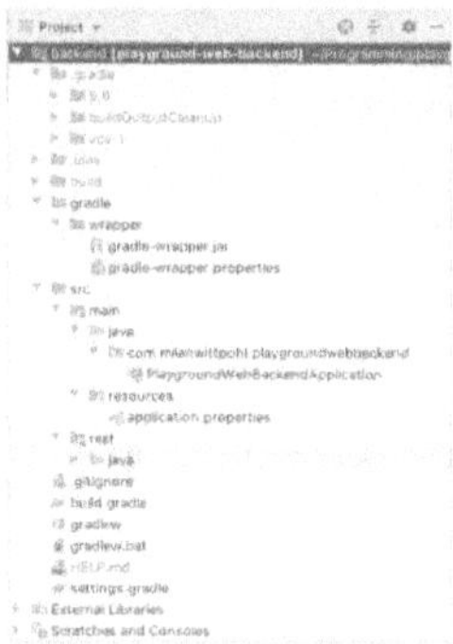

To do that, we need to understand every folder and file contained in the root directory:

.gradle – This is the Gradle cache. For example, when Gradle resolves a dependency, it is cached in this folder.

.idea – This stores the project settings and has nothing in it right now.

build – When the project is run, this folder is created and stores the java classes that have been compiled. These are then loaded into JVM so the project can run.

gradle – You cannot use Gradle without the gradle-wrapper. This provides the required Gradle build.

src – This stores the source code. Shortly, we will look at a generated file called PlaygroundWebBackendApplication.java

.gitignore – This is where the directories and files that must not be included in git are stored.

build.gradle – This contains four separate sections:

- Plugins – Gradle plugins extend the project's capabilities. They can extend Gradle, configure your project, and apply a specific configuration.

We are using three plugins:

- Spring Boot – Lets us use Gradle to build a Spring Boot application. Without it, Gradle would not have the means to build the project.

- Spring Dependency Management – Lets us define the dependencies without needing to provide any version numbers. The plugin matches the Spring Boot version with those dependencies.

- Java – As you would expect, this lets us use Gradle to build a Java project.

Metadata – The group and version sections are self-explanatory, and the source compatibility tells you the compatible version of Java for your source code.

Repositories – This is where we let Gradle know where it should look for the defined dependencies.

Dependencies – This is where Gradle is informed of the required dependencies and asked to retrieve them. Every dependency will have two parts – the dependency and the configuration. The dependency name is self-explanatory, but the configuration deserves a deeper look. The configuration informs Gradle of the purpose for the dependency, and the

Java plugin provides these. Most of the time, implementation will be used as the dependency is typically only used to implement the program.

Gradlew – This is a shell script that starts the gradle-wrapper on Unix and macOS systems.

gradlew.bat – This is a shell script that starts the gradle-wrapper on a Windows system.

HELP.md – This is a help text file generated by the Spring Initializer.

settings.gradle – This is where the Gradle settings are set.

Before we actually begin to program, let's look at that file we mentioned earlier. The PlaygroundWebBackendApplication.java file is a Java Source File, and it has 14 lines of code:

package com.(your project name).playgroundwebbackend;

import org.springframework.boot.SpringApplication;

```java
import
org.springframework.boot.autoconfigure.Spri
ngBootApplication;

@SpringBootApplication

public                                  class
PlaygroundWebBackendApplication {

public static void main(String[] args) {

SpringApplication.run(PlaygroundWebBacken
dApplication.class, args);

}

}
```

Most of this is fairly self-explanatory, but you might have spotted a strange annotation - @SpringBootApplication. You will see many annotations like this in Spring, and we'll look at some later. Typically, annotations are used in Java as interpreted markers. Spring will examine your files and apply the appropriate logic.

As far as @SpringBootApplication goes, here's what it does. That one annotation takes the place of three more:

- @EnableAutoConfiguration examines your applications, does its checks and assumptions, and ensures your application has the standard configuration required to run.

- @ComponentScan indicates where to look to find classes with the Spring annotations.

- @Configuration informs Spring that the class is used for the configuration.

Okay, that was quite a lot to take in. Take a bit of time to understand, and then we will move on to the next part – setting up a simple endpoint, just to give you an idea of what it's all about. Then we will connect a database and ensure our app is secure.

Adding a single endpoint – so that you can understand it

The first thing we need to do is tell Spring that we need web functionalities developed. Doing that is as simple as altering the dependencies listed in the build.gradle file:

```
dependencies {

implementation 'org.springframework.boot:spring-boot-starter-web'

testImplementation 'org.springframework.boot:spring-boot-starter-test'

}
```

Adding the -web suffix allows us access to more libraries. Once the dependencies have been reimported, we can begin to code.

Before we get to that, you need to know that, in Spring, an endpoint is called a controller.

Spring uses the Spring Web MVC Framework, the data served up by the application. It could be a web page we use Spring to render. The model is referenced, sending the data to the controller, and the view is given the required information. Because Spring isn't used for rendering views, we don't get one. As such, the controller is the endpoint as it responds to the web request.

Defining a new controller requires we create two things:

- A new package named controller

- A new Java class named HelloWorldCreator

And defining an endpoint requires three things:

1. The new class must be declared as a controller

Spring needs to know that HelloWorldController is, in fact, a controller. This is done using a stereotype annotation and there are two that can be used to define controllers - @Controller and @RestController.

@RestController is an @Controller specialization used to make implementing the setup a little easier. This is because the @ResponseBody annotation does not need to be explicitly added to the endpoints. Quite simply, the annotation is added to the class:

@RestController

public class HelloWorldController {}

2. Then, we create the endpoint

This is simple enough to do – we just need to define a method. It can call different classes and return any object type. Keeping things simple, we will return a String:

Chapter 14: Java With Maven

This chapter will use Maven to build a simple Java project to explain how it all works. We'll create a simple application that tells us what the time is and then build it using Maven.

It will take you about 15 minutes, and all you need is your IDE and the JDK.

Like many guides in getting started with Spring, you can do one of two things – start from scratch or download the code from an alternative repository. We're going to start from scratch:

Step One

First is setting up a Java project so Maven can build it. We'll keep this very simple for now, and you can create this in any project folder you choose.

Step Two

Once your project directory is set up, create a sub-directory structure as follows.

└── src

└── main

└── java

└── hello

In the src/main/java/hello directory, Java classes can be created, any that you want. For this guide, we'll create two – HelloWorld.java and Greeter.java.

src/main/java/hello/HelloWorld.java

package hello;

public class HelloWorld {

public static void main(String[] args) {

Greeter greeter = new Greeter();

System.out.println(greeter.sayHello());

}

}COPY

src/main/java/hello/Greeter.java

package hello;

public class Greeter {

public String sayHello() {

return "Hello world!";

}

}COPY

STEP THREE

Your project is ready for Maven to build so, now, you need Maven installed.

Open https://maven.apache.org/download.cgi. Maven is a zip file, so look for a link that says apache-maven-{version} — bin.zip pr bin.tar.gz.

Download the file and unzip it, saving it where you can easily access it.

The bin folder needs to be added to your path, and then you can open the command line and test the installation:

mvn -v

If it is all okay, you should see information regarding your Maven installation, something similar to this:

Apache Maven 3.3.9 (bb52d8502b132ec0a5a3f4c09453c07478323dc5; 2015-11-10T16:41:47+00:00)

Maven home: /home/dsyer/Programs/apache-maven

Java version: 1.8.0_152, vendor: Azul Systems, Inc.

Java home: /home/dsyer/.sdkman/candidates/java/8u152-zulu/jre

Default locale: en_GB, platform encoding: UTF-8

OS name: "linux", version: "4.15.0-36-generic", arch: "amd64", family: "unix"

Maven is successfully installed.

STEP FOUR

Time to create the definition of your Maven project. These are defined using an XML file called pom.xml. This file provides the name and version of your project and the dependencies on external libraries.

Start by creatinga file at the project's root and call it pom.xml. Make sure it is places next to the folder called src and input the following into it:

pom.xml

<?xml version="1.0" encoding="UTF-8"?>

<project
xmlns="http://maven.apache.org/POM/4.0.0"
xmlns:xsi="your   group   or
organization/2001/XMLSchema-instance"

xsi:schemaLocation="http://maven.apache.or
g/POM/4.0.0
https://maven.apache.org/xsd/maven-
4.0.0.xsd">

```xml
<modelVersion>4.0.0</modelVersion>

<groupId>org.springframework</groupId>

<artifactId>gs-maven</artifactId>

<packaging>jar</packaging>

<version>0.1.0</version>

<properties>

<maven.compiler.source>1.8</maven.compiler.source>

<maven.compiler.target>1.8</maven.compiler.target>

</properties>

<build>

<plugins>

<plugin>

<groupId>org.apache.maven.plugins</groupId>

<artifactId>maven-shade-plugin</artifactId>
```

```xml
<version>3.2.4</version>

<executions>

<execution>

<phase>package</phase>

<goals>

<goal>shade</goal>

</goals>

<configuration>

<transformers>

<transformer

implementation="org.apache.maven.plugins.shade.resource.ManifestResourceTransformer
">

<mainClass>hello.HelloWorld</mainClass>

</transformer>

</transformers>
</configuration>
```

```
</execution>

</executions>

</plugin>

</plugins>

</build>

</project>COPY
```

The <packaging> element is optional and, besides that, this is the simplest form of the pom.xml file you need to build your project in Java. The following details about the project's configuration are included:

- <modelVersion> - The model version of POM, which is always 4.0.0

- <groupID> - The organization or group that own the project, more often expressed as a domain name (inverted)

- <artifactID> - The name being provided to the library artifact for the project – i.e., the name given to the WAR and JAR file

- <version> - The version of the project you are building

- <packaging> - Details how to package the project. The default is jar but, if you want WAR file packaging, change it to war.

Spring recommends using the semantic approach for choosing versioning schemes.

Right now, you have a very simple, minimal Maven Project.

Step Five

Maven is now set up and ready for you to build your project. You can now use Maven to execute build-lifecycle goals, including those to compile the code, create library packages, install libraries in the dependency repository, and so on.

Try your build by inputting the following command at the command line:

mvn compile

Maven will run as the command has told it to execute your goal to compile the file. Look in the target/classes directory when it's done, where you will see the compiled .class files.

It's not likely that you will need to work with or distribute .class files directly, so, instead, we'll run the package goal:

mvn package

This will compile the code, run necessary tests, and, to finish, packages the code in a JAR file and puts it in the target directory. The JAR file name is based on the <artifactId> and <version>. For example, given the small POM file we built, it will be called gs-maven-0.1.0.jar.

The following code should be executed to run the file:

java -jar target/gs-maven-0.1.0.jar

If you change the <packaging> value from jar to war, you will see a WAR file instead of a JAR file in the directory.

Maven will also keep a repository containing the dependencies stored on your local machine.It is usually in a directory called xxx.m2/repository in your home directory, and it provides you with easy access to your project's dependencies. If you want to install the JAR file to that repository, you need the install goal invoked:

mvn install

The goal compiles and tests the code, packaging it and copying it to the local repository for dependencies. That way, it can be referenced as a dependency by other projects.

Step Six

It's now time to declare the dependencies in our Maven build.The Hello World sample is self-contained, not depending on any other libraries. However, most applications do depend on other libraries when they need complex or common functionalities handled.

Let's say, for example, that as well as saying "Hello World!," you want the date and time printed too. You could use the facilities provided for in the native Java libraries, but you could also make things that bit more exciting by using the Joda Time libraries.

First, HelloWorld.java needs to be changed, so it looks like this:

src/main/java/hello/HelloWorld.java

```java
package hello;

import org.joda.time.LocalTime;

public class HelloWorld {

public static void main(String[] args) {

LocalTime currentTime = new LocalTime();

System.out.println("The current local time is: " + currentTime);

Greeter greeter = new Greeter();

System.out.println(greeter.sayHello());
```

}

}COPY

HelloWorld is using the LocalTime class in Joda Time to get the current time and print it.

If you built the project by running mvn compile, it would fail. Why? Because Joda Time has not been declared in the build as a compile dependency. That is easily fixed by including the following lines, inside the <project> element, in your pom.xml file:

<dependencies>

<dependency>

<groupId>joda-time</groupId>

<artifactId>joda-time</artifactId>

<version>2.9.2</version>

</dependency>

</dependencies>COPY

This XML block declares the project's dependencies, specifically, one dependency related to the Joda Time library. Inside the <dependency> element, three sub-elements are used to define the dependency coordinates:

- <groupId> - indicates the organization or group owning the dependency

- <artifactId> - indicates the required library

- <version> - indicates the specific library version required

By default, every dependency is scoped as a compile dependency. That means they are (or should be) available when it comes to compile time. You can also specify a <scope> element so you can specify a particular scope:

- provided — these are the dependencies needed to compile the code but are provided by a container at runtime. The container runs the code, for example, a Java Servlet API.

- test — these are the dependencies need to compile and run tests but are not needed to build or run the runtime code.

If you were to run mvn package or mvn compile now, the Joda Time dependency should be resolved from the central repository, and you will have a successful

Chapter 15: Java With Gradle

This chapter will walk you through getting to know Gradle by building a simple app. It will take about 15 minutes, and all you need is the JDK and an IDE.

As with the Maven guide, you can start from scratch or download the code from an external source – we are starting from scratch.

Step One

First, we need to create a new Java project to build with Gradle. We'll keep it simple for now so, go ahead and do that.

Step Two

Next, we create the directory structure. Do this in your choice of project directory – create a subdirectory as follows:

└── src

└── main

└── java

└── hello

You can create whatever Java classes you like in the src/main/java/hello directory. We'll create the same two classes we did with the Maven guide – HelloWorld.java and Greeter.java

src/main/java/hello/HelloWorld.java

```java
package hello;

public class HelloWorld {

public static void main(String[] args) {

Greeter greeter = new Greeter();

System.out.println(greeter.sayHello());

}

}COPY
```

src/main/java/hello/Greeter.java

```java
package hello;

public class Greeter {
```

```java
public String sayHello() {

return "Hello world!";

}

}COPY
```

Step Three

Now we can go ahead and install Gradle. To do this, we recommend you use an installer:

- SDKMAN

- Homebrew (brew install gradle)

If neither of these works for you, the binaries can be downloaded from https://www.gradle.org/downloads. You only require the binaries, so find the gradle-version-bin.zip file. Alternatively, choose the gradle-version-all.zip if you want the documentation and sources too.

Unzip and save the file to your computer and make sure the bin folder is added to your path.

Test the installation by running Gradle from your command line:

gradle

If all is well, you will see something similar to the following:

:help

Welcome to Gradle 6.0.1.

To run a build, run gradle <task> ...

To see a list of available tasks, run gradle tasks

To see a list of command-line options, run gradle --help

To see more detail about a task, run gradle help --task <task>

For troubleshooting, visit https://help.gradle.org

Deprecated Gradle features were used in this build, making it incompatible with Gradle 7.0.

Use '--warning-mode all' to show the individual deprecation warnings.

See https://docs.gradle.org/6.0.1/userguide/command_line_interface.html#sec:command_line _warnings

BUILD SUCCESSFUL in 455ms

1 actionable task: 1 executed

Gradle is successfully installed.

Now you can explore to see what it can do. Before you go ahead and create a .gradle project, find out what tasks there are:

gradle tasks

A list of the available tasks should appear on your screen. Assuming Gradle was run in a folder that doesn't contain a build.gradle file already, what you will see are elementary tasks, such as:

:tasks

Tasks runnable from root project

Build Setup tasks

----

init - Initializes a new Gradle build.

wrapper - Generates Gradle wrapper files.

Help tasks

----

buildEnvironment - Displays all buildscript dependencies declared in root project 'gs-gradle'.

components - Displays the components produced by root project 'gs-gradle'. [incubating]

dependencies - Displays all dependencies declared in root project 'gs-gradle'.

dependencyInsight - Displays the insight into a specific dependency in root project 'gs-gradle'.

dependentComponents - Displays the dependent components of components in root project 'gs-gradle'. [incubating]

help - Displays a help message.

model - Displays the configuration model of root project 'gs-gradle'. [incubating]

outgoingVariants - Displays the outgoing variants of root project 'gs-gradle'.

projects - Displays the sub-projects of root project 'gs-gradle'.

properties - Displays the properties of root project 'gs-gradle'.

tasks - Displays the tasks runnable from root project 'gs-gradle'.

To see all tasks and more detail, run gradle tasks --all

To see more detail about a task, run gradle help --task <task>

Deprecated Gradle features were used in this build, making it incompatible with Gradle 7.0.

Use '--warning-mode all' to show the individual deprecation warnings.

See https://docs.gradle.org/6.0.1/userguide/command_line_interface.html#sec:command_line_warnings

BUILD SUCCESSFUL in 477ms

1 actionable task: 1 executed

Although these tasks are there, without a build configuration, they are not much value. As you flesh out the build.gradle file, you will find some of the tasks are of more use. And as plugins are added to the file, that task list will continue to grow, so it would be helpful if you ran the command occasionally to see what's been added.

Step Four

We want to build our code and do this by adding a plugin that gives us basic build functionality.

Start by building a simple build.gradle file inside your <project folder>, the one you created right at the start. Add a single line of code to it:

apply plugin: 'java'COPY

It may only be one line, but it is very powerful. Try running gradle tasks again, and you will see that some new tasks have been added to the list. That includes those to build a project, create JavaDoc and run tests.

Gradle build will often be used because it compiles the code, tests it, and assembles it into a JAR file. It is run with this command:

gradle build

Give it a few seconds, and you should see a message saying, BUILD SUCCESSFUL. That indicates your build has finished.

Look in the build folder to see the build results, and you should find some directories. Three of those are:

- classes – these are the .class files compiled for the project

- reports – these reports are produced by your build and including things like test reports

- libs – these are the assembled libraries for the project and are usually WAR and WAR files.

Inside the classes folder, you will find the .class files that come from the Java code being compiled.Two specific files you should find are HelloWorld.class and Greeter.class.

Your project won't have any library dependencies right now, so you shouldn't see anything in the dependency_cache folder.

In the reports folder, you will see a report containing details of the project's running unit tests – not the most interesting of reports to read.

You will see a JAR file with the same name as the project folder in the libs folder. A bit later, you will see how the JAR name and version can be specified.

Step Five

Time to declare our dependencies. Our HelloWorld sample is self-contained, with no dependencies on external libraries. However, most applications need external libraries for complex or common functionality.

As we did with our Maven project, you might want to see the data and time, as well as Hello World!. Again, we will use the Joda Time libraries for this, so change HelloWorld.java, so it looks like this:

package hello;

import org.joda.time.LocalTime;

```
public class HelloWorld {

public static void main(String[] args) {

LocalTime currentTime = new LocalTime();

System.out.println("The current local time is:
" + currentTime);

Greeter greeter = new Greeter();

System.out.println(greeter.sayHello());

}

}COPY
```

The LocalTime class in Joda Time is used to get the current time and print it. Again, this build would fail because Joda Time has not been declared as a compile dependency.

To start with, a source needs to be added for third-party libraries:

```
repositories {

mavenCentral()

}COPY
```

This code block indicates that the build should use the Maven Central Repository to resolve dependencies. Gradle is heavily reliant on many of the facilities and conventions the Maven build tool establishes, including using Maven Central as a dependency source.